POLAR
ANIMAL GROUPS

by
Rebecca Phillips-Bartlett

Minneapolis, Minnesota

Credits
All images are courtesy of Shutterstock.com, unless otherwise specified. With thanks to Getty Images, Thinkstock Photo, and iStockphoto. Recurring images – happpy.designer, KosOlga, piixypeach, AnnstasAg, Ihor Biliavskyi. Cover Images – Eric Isselee, Roger ARPS BPE1 CPAGB, polarma, slowmotiongli, evaurban. 2–3 – evaurban. 4–5 – Sergey Krasnoshchokovi, Lua Carlos Martins. 6–7 – Armin Rose, Troutnut, vladsilver, outdoorsman, Matis75. 8–9 – Sergey Uryadnikov, AndreAnita, Himanshu Saraf, Agami Photo Agency. 10–11 – Vladimir Melnik, slowmotiongli, AnnstasAg, Dolores M. Harvey, karenfoleyphotography. 12–13 – Ondrej Prosicky, tryton2011, Zaruba Ondrej, Guz Anna, NotionPic. 14–15 – Robert Adrian Hillman, longtaildog, Robert Haasmann, AnnstasAg, Mircea Costina. 16–17 – Jim Cumming, Josef_Svoboda, Timothy Stringer, DGIM studio. 18–19 – Mircea Costina, Breck P. Kent, AnnstasAg, derekmorganphotography, rooh183. 20–21 – BMJ, vladsilver, AnnstasAg, NotionPic. 22–23 – GUDKOV ANDREY, karl umbriaco, Maksym Drozd.

Bearport Publishing Company Product Development Team
President: Jen Jenson; Director of Product Development: Spencer Brinker; Managing Editor: Allison Juda; Associate Editor: Naomi Reich; Associate Editor: Tiana Tran; Senior Designer: Colin O'Dea; Associate Designer: Elena Klinkner; Associate Designer: Kayla Eggert; Product Development Assistant: Owen Hamlin

Library of Congress Cataloging-in-Publication Data

Names: Phillips-Bartlett, Rebecca, 1999- author.
Title: Polar animal groups / by Rebecca Phillips-Bartlett.
Description: Minneapolis, Minnesota : Bearport Publishing Company, [2024] | Series: Wild animal families | Includes index.
Identifiers: LCCN 2023030605 (print) | LCCN 2023030606 (ebook) | ISBN 9798889163220 (library binding) | ISBN 9798889163275 (paperback) | ISBN 9798889163312 (ebook)
Subjects: LCSH: Animals--Polar regions--Juvenile literature.
Classification: LCC QL104 .P53 2024 (print) | LCC QL104 (ebook) | DDC 591.0911--dc23/eng/20230710
LC record available at https://lccn.loc.gov/2023030605
LC ebook record available at https://lccn.loc.gov/2023030606

© 2024 BookLife Publishing
This edition is published by arrangement with BookLife Publishing.

North American adaptations © 2024 Bearport Publishing Company. All rights reserved. No part of this publication may be reproduced in whole or in part, stored in any retrieval system, or transmitted in any form or by any means, electronic, mechanical, photocopying, recording, or otherwise, without written permission from the publisher.

For more information, write to Bearport Publishing, 5357 Penn Avenue South, Minneapolis, MN 55419.

CONTENTS

Wild Animal Families.......... 4
In the Polar Regions.......... 6
Polar Bears 8
Harp Seals 10
Walruses 12
Caribou..................... 14
Arctic Wolves............... 16
Arctic Foxes 18
Emperor Penguins............ 20
Family Focus................ 22
Glossary.................... 24
Index 24

WILD ANIMAL FAMILIES

Earth is full of amazing animals. Many of them live in groups. This helps animals stay safe. It also makes it easier for them to find food and a place to stay.

Many different animal families live in cold parts of the world.

Let's visit different animal families in the **polar regions**. The **habitats** there are harsh, but many still call it home.

IN THE POLAR REGIONS

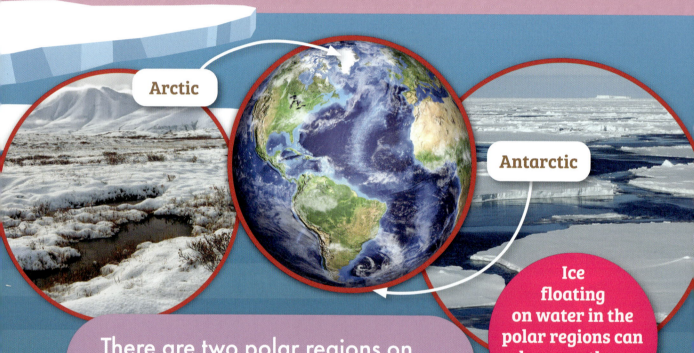

Arctic

Antarctic

There are two polar regions on Earth. The Arctic is at the very north of the world. It is around the North Pole. The Antarctic is in the far south by the South Pole.

Ice floating on water in the polar regions can be more than 10 feet (3 m) thick.

The Arctic and Antarctic are both very cold. The animals that live in these **environments** have **adapted** to this weather. Some animals live in groups to make life in the cold easier and safer.

POLAR BEARS

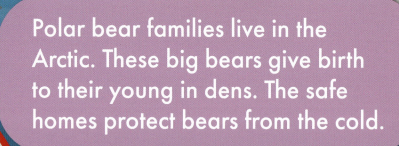

Polar bear families live in the Arctic. These big bears give birth to their young in dens. The safe homes protect bears from the cold.

A mother bear will make a hole at the top of her den for air.

Polar bear cubs live with their mother for about two years. During this time, the mother teaches her cubs how to hunt. The bear family sits near open water and catches seals that come out of the water.

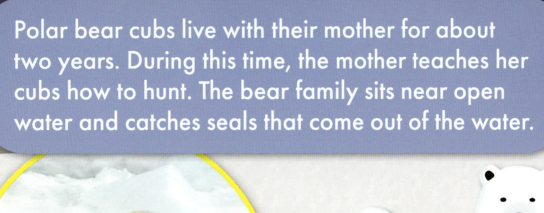

A bear family waiting for a meal

HARP SEALS

Harp seals spend most of their time in the water. But they go up on ice when they are getting ready to have babies. On the ice, they live in large groups called colonies.

Baby harp seals are white for about two weeks after they are born. Then, they turn gray.

Harp seals also gather when they **migrate**. Groups of more than a thousand travel together at different times of the year. The seals work together to hunt along the way.

WALRUSES

Walruses live in large groups called herds. They **communicate** with one another using loud bellows and snorts. If one walrus senses danger, it rushes to the water. The rest of the herd hurries to follow.

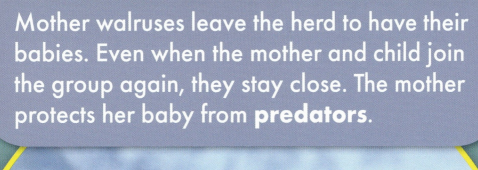

Mother walruses leave the herd to have their babies. Even when the mother and child join the group again, they stay close. The mother protects her baby from **predators**.

When in danger, walrus mothers pick up their babies and dive into the water.

CARIBOU

Caribou live in groups. They often gather together with tens to hundreds of animals. When it is time to migrate, they join together in large herds with thousands of caribou.

Caribou migrate more than 600 miles (970 km).

Caribou live and travel in herds to protect one another from harm. They have a stinky way to keep safe. Special **glands** on their ankles give off a warning smell when there is danger.

ARCTIC WOLVES

Arctic wolves live in packs. Working as a group helps wolves hunt animals that are much bigger than they are.

Living in groups also lets young wolves learn from older members of the pack. One skill they learn is howling. This helps wolves in the pack communicate.

Howling also warns other wolf packs to stay away.

ARCTIC FOXES

Arctic foxes live in dens. Some of these homes pass from one family of foxes to another, and then another for hundreds of years.

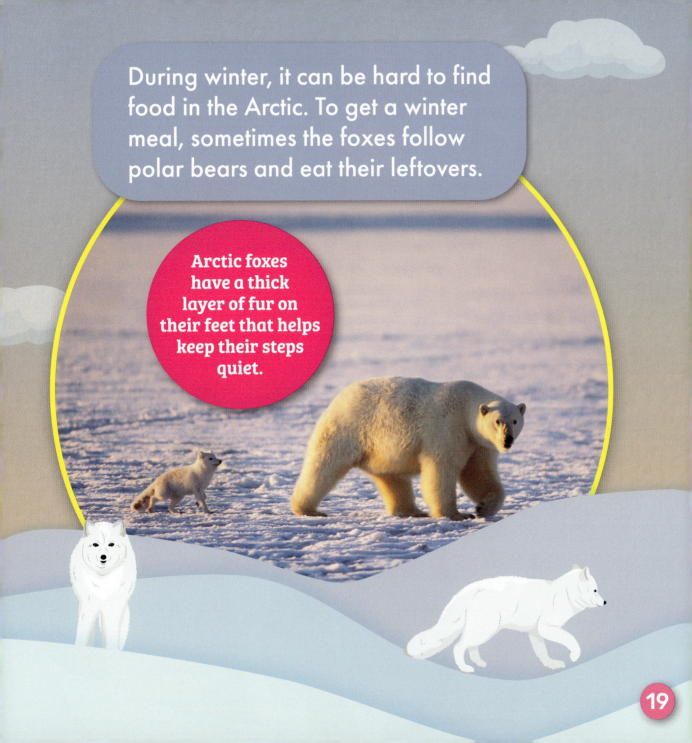

During winter, it can be hard to find food in the Arctic. To get a winter meal, sometimes the foxes follow polar bears and eat their leftovers.

Arctic foxes have a thick layer of fur on their feet that helps keep their steps quiet.

EMPEROR PENGUINS

Emperor penguins live in the Antarctic. When it is time to have babies, they gather in large colonies. There can be as many as to 10,000 penguins in one colony.

Penguins huddle together to keep warm.

Young penguins in the colony gather in groups called crèches (KRESH-iz) while their parents hunt. When they come back with food, the parents find their baby among more than 100 baby penguins.

Penguins in a crèche

FAMILY FOCUS

Many amazing family groups live in the polar regions. These groups are all different in many ways. However, they do have some things in common.

GLOSSARY

adapted changed to survive in the environment

communicate to share information

environments the plants, animals, and weather in places

glands body parts that make something useful or do a special job

habitats places in nature where plants or animals normally live

migrate to move from one place to another at a certain time of the year

polar regions the icy areas near the North Pole or South Pole

predators animals that hunt and eat other animals

INDEX

Antarctic 6–7, 20
Arctic 6–8, 16, 19
colonies 10, 20–21
cubs 9

dens 8, 18
habitats 5, 23
herds 12–15

migrate 11, 14, 23
mothers 8–9, 13, 21
packs 16–17